Fruit of a mahonia.

Clematis hybrid.

The author
Gerhard Worm studied garden design at the School for Garden Design in Berlin-Dahlem. Since 1983 he has worked as a garden and plant consultant on the island of Mainau. As head of department, he is responsible for seminars, and teaching about nature, environmental protection and organic gardening.
He is the author of the successful title 'Roses' in this series.

The photographers
Jürgen Becker, Ursel Borstell, Marion Nickig and Hans Reinhard have all spent years working for well-known specialist periodicals and book publishing companies. Further photos are by other well-known plant photographers (see Acknowledgements, page 63).

The illustrator
Renate Holzner works as a freelance illustrator and graphic artist for well-known publishing companies and agencies. Her repertoire extends from line drawings to photo-realistic illustrations and computer graphics.

Important: Please read the 'Author's notes' on page 63 so that you can fully enjoy your ornamental shrubs and trees.

Success with

Jasmine, lilac

and other ornamental shrubs and trees

GERHARD WORM

MURDOCH
B O O K S

Introduction and Contents

Ornamental shrubs and trees are the backbone of any successful garden design. They help to form proper divisions, with the right kind of artistic tension, and create atmospheric, secluded corners. They dispense welcome shade, but also protect you from curious glances, as well as from wind, dust and street noise. In addition, shrubs will disguise less attractive views and provide an environment for a host of living creatures. Their brilliant flowers, colourful fruits, evergreen leaves or splendid autumn colouring and their great variety of shapes and forms of growth will create an everlasting series of new vistas throughout the course of the year. This book will introduce you to the most beautiful shrubs and trees. Stunning photographs give you an idea of their multitude of shapes and colours. Shrub and tree expert Gerhard Worm practically demonstrates the best way to design and plant your garden, and he gives examples of some typical situations. Detailed tables will help you to choose appropriate plant species. Expert information about care and propagating is also provided. Clear and simple illustrations help to explain the most important steps.

Beautiful shapes and colours with hydrangeas.

A colourful variety

Shrubs and trees give a garden structure and are, therefore, counted among its most indispensable elements. Their flowers, leaves and fruits provide many highlights throughout the year. The following pages recommend the best types of shrubs and trees and explain the many ways in which they can be used.

Top: Roses – here a Bourbon rose – are among the most profusely flowering of ornamental shrubs. Some also have a wonderful scent.
Left: Azaleas and rhododendrons unfold their intensely colourful blooms on acid soil.

A colourful variety

Ornamental shrubs and trees in the garden

Ornamental shrubs and trees are species that have woody stems but are not exactly 'useful', in the sense that they are not edible. Instead, they have an attractive appearance and play an important part in the garden in other ways:

● With their size and long lifespan, they provide the main framework for any garden design.

● They create separate spaces and divide up the garden.

● They provide colour, many different shapes and some wonderful scents in planted areas.

● They form boundaries between the garden and the outside.

● They form an attractive, protective screen against curious onlookers, and against noise, dust and wind.

● In the summer, they provide shade.

● They help disguise less attractive areas.

● They provide living space and nourishment for many living creatures.

● Planted on a slope, they hold on to the soil with their roots and protect the ground from erosion.

A great variety of shrubs and trees

Just a few ornamental shrubs and trees will turn a bare and barren area into a comfortable 'green living room'.

Solitary shrubs and trees (see page 26) are conspicuous species that create an attractive, eyecatching feature, when they stand alone.

Groups of shrubs and trees (see page 26) look good when combined with others.

Climbing shrubs (see page 8) cover walls, trelisses and espaliers with greenery, provide a visual screen and do not require much space.

Ground-covering species (see page 8) grow low and spread. They subdue weed growth and make an attractive underplanting.

Deciduous shrubs and trees (see table page 14) lose their leaves in the autumn or winter and allow more light into the garden. Before that, they display a splendid range of colours.

Evergreen shrubs (see table page 19) will provide colour and a visual screen, even on grey winter days. They do not lose their leaves or needles in the autumn, but replace them constantly throughout the whole year, whenever required. Evergreen leaves are sensitive to drying out as they lose water through evaporation.

Coniferous shrubs (see table page 19) form needles instead of leaves. With the exception of the larch (*Larix* species), they belong among the evergreens and do not have any conspicuous flowers. They can look rather gloomy or boring when planted in larger groups.

Shrubs and trees that can stand cutting (see page 30 to 33) can be turned into narrow hedges, edging or miniature works of topiary art.

Small gardens

Plant small or very slow-growing species in small gardens, to prevent overcrowding. Many of them can be kept for years in containers on your patio or in your courtyard.

Easy to care for or not?

Do you simply want to enjoy your garden and relax in it, or do you like gardening so much that you want to work regularly at gardening as a pleasant, consuming hobby?

● If you want an easy to care for garden, you need to plant more evergreen plants, because they grow slowly, as a rule, and will not require much cutting. They do not lose much foliage that needs raking up. You will also save time and effort if you choose species that thrive in the type of soil you have in your garden. Give preference to hardy shrubs that will not require a lot of time and effort spent on winter protection. In general, indigenous shrubs, or those that derive from similar climatic zones, will be a great deal less demanding and more robust than exotic species. They will not

Lilac is very attractive as a solitary shrub or in a group.

be so susceptible to infestation and will require hardly any fertilizer. A layer of mulch will decrease the need for care (see page 45), as it will subdue 'weeds'. Ground-cover plants like lesser periwinkle (*Vinca minor*) and St John's wort (*Hypericum claycinum*) will fulfil the same function.

The more labour-intensive garden will sport more decorative deciduous shrubs and trees. Depending on the vigour of their growth, they will have to be cut regularly to keep them in shape and encourage them to form new flowers. After a few years, a rejuvenating cut will also be necessary (see **Practise:** Cutting, pages 50–1). The dead leaves will have to be swept up every autumn. This means more work!

Hedges that are kept in shape, or a formal garden, will require a great deal of effort. The latter will, however, look particularly beautiful (see photos, page 33). The garden will also require additional work and effort if you decide to collect exotic, rare shrubs.

My tip: Make do without the kinds of shrub that require changes to the consistency of the soil, in order to maintain the ecologically valuable micro-soil organisms.

Practise: botany

Shrubs grow shoots that, unlike those of herbaceous plants, become woody and do not die in the winter. These solid, woody shoots, may eventually develop into mighty tree tops.

Shapes of growth
Illustration 1

Among the shrubs are counted trees, bushes and semi-bushes, as well as many climbing and ground-covering plants.
Trees form a trunk that, in contrast to a bush, does not branch out until it reaches a certain height. The branches and twigs form a species-characteristic crown. The crown may be round, oval or heart-shaped (see illustration 1b) or pillar-like (see illustration 1c).
Bushes (see illustration 1d) like the rose (*Rosa* species) have branches that spread out just above the ground. Bushes remain much shorter than trees.
Semi-bushes like sage (*Salvia officinalis*) will

only become woody in their lower parts, and the tips of the shoots will die off in winter.
Ground-covering species (see illustration 1e) like the dwarf cotoneaster (*Cotoneaster* species) or the lesser periwinkle (*Vinca minor*) may grow across large areas with their numerous creeping or low-growing, upright runners. They will protect the soil from drying out and subdue 'weeds'.
Climbing shrubs (see illustration 1f) will grow woody, but require some support in order to grow upright. Each species has a different method of climbing:

● *Rambling plants,* like the climbing rose (*Rosa* species), will hold onto climbing aids with their thorns. Tying them to the support will help.
● *Winding plants* like the wisteria (*Wisteria* species, left-winding species that climb by turning anti-clockwise) or honeysuckle (*Lonicera* species, clockwise winding) grow like lianas by winding entire shoots around the climbing support.
● *Plants with tendrils*, like clematis (*Clematis* species), form tendrils out of leaf stalks, shoots or feathery leaves, that wrap around a support like gripping arms.

● *Plants with root suckers* like ivy (*Hedera helix*) and the climbing hydrangea (*Hydrangea anomala ssp. petiolaris*) form adhering roots and can use these to climb up walls without any further support.
● *Adhesive pads* are formed by the self-climbing Virginia creeper (*Parthenocissus tricuspidata*) which can also manage without any climbing aids.

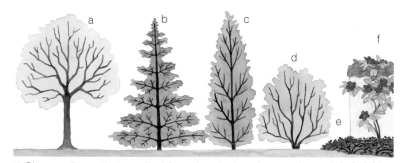

1 Shapes of growth: trees (a-c) branch out when they reach a certain height, bushes (d) begin just above the ground. Ground-covering plants (e) grow horizontally, climbing plants (f) grow vertically on a support.

2a A plant with male and female flowers on two different bushes: example holly.

2b Male and female flowers on the same bush: example hazel.

2c Plant with male and female sexual organs in one flower: example rose.

Flowers and fruits
Illustrations 2a–c

Flowers serve as a means to multiply and ensure the survival of the species. For seeds to form, the flower has to be fertilized by pollen being carried from the stamens to the stigma. Pollination is generally carried out by insects. Flowers are either conspicuous, strongly scented, or they offer nectar in order to lure insects. Conifers or the hazel (*Corylus avellana*) rely on the wind for pollination. They form numerous, inconspicuous flowers for the purpose.

Hermaphrodite flowers
The majority of ornamental shrubs, like the rose (*Rosa majalis*, see illustration 2c) are hermaphrodite, that is,

they comprise male (stamens) and female sexual organs (stigma with ovary). After pollination, this species forms red rosehips. Many new, double varieties are, however, infertile.

Single sex flowers
They do not have either the pollen receptacles or the ovary.
● Plants that form separate male and female flowers on one individual plant. Among these are the hazelnut (*Corylus avellana*, see illustration 2b).
● Plants that form male flowers on one plant and female flowers on another. Among these are the holly (*Ilex aquifolium*, see illustration 2a) and sea buckthorn (*Hippophae rhamnoides*). If you

want berries from these, you will need to plant both female and male specimens.

Grafting and wild shoots
Illustration 3

Many ornamental shrubs are offered as 'grafted varieties'. This means that the variety has been grafted onto a related species. The partner with its roots in the ground is the stock, and the grafted variety forms the part that is above ground. Where both partners are joined together, you will be able to see a clearly visible knobble. Grafted plants offer the following advantages:
● Many species can only be propagated in this way.

● Growth and resistance to disease can be favourably influenced in this way. Grafted varieties may need special care:
● As with roses, wild shoots will form below the grafting point. They grow vigorously, rob the plant of its strength and should be cut off.
● The grafting point will often require winter protection (see page 57).

3 Grafting and formation of wild shoots in grafted roses.

9

A colourful variety

Position

Ornamental shrubs have different requirements and characteristics and you should find out about these before purchasing any plants.

Soil. A humus-rich, porous soil is ideal (see page 44). You may wish to improve your soil, if it does not match this ideal (see page 45). This often quite complicated process will not be necessary if you choose very robust shrubs, such as laburnum (*Laburnum* species) or the pea tree (*Caragana arborescens*), that manage in any soil.

● *Lime content.* Some shrubs, like rhododendron, do not like any lime or chalk in the soil; others love it, like the yew (*Taxus* species, see table, page 19 and text pages 29 and 31).
The calcium content of your garden soil can also be altered (see page 45).

● *Dryness.* A few shrubs will flourish in very dry positions: among these are the butterfly tree (*Buddleia* species) and spiraea (*Caryopteris x clandonensis*). Periwinkles are not very suitable for these positions, as they require water even in winter. Naturally, you can still plant species that require more moisture in dry positions, but you will have to water them a lot.

Light. Ornamental shrubs thrive in plenty of sunshine. Some may manage with semi-shade, such as the hydrangea (*Hydrangea* species and hybrids), the Cornelian cherry (*Cornus mas*), and a very few will even cope with shade, such as box (*Buxus sempervirens*).

Temperature. Ornamental shrubs usually prefer a warm position, protected from wind. Very warmth-loving species should be planted in front of a protective wall, if possible. If your garden is in a hollow, in which cold air tends to collect, only plant very robust bushes.

Resistance to frost. Preferably choose ornamental shrubs from indigenous tree nurseries, that have proven themselves to be hardy in your climate. More sensitive shrubs will require winter protection (see page 57).

Hardiness to fumes. In cities, traffic fumes and dust may affect shrubs a great deal. Species that are green only in the summer cope more easily, as they lose their foliage every year and detoxify themselves in this way. The following species will cope quite well with pollution, and the expert denotes them with the term 'pollution-hardy':

Among conifers these are the false cypress (*Chamaecyparis* species), juniper (*Juniperus* species), yew (*Taxus* species) and cedar or arbor-vitae (*Thuja* species). Among the deciduous shrubs these are snowy mespilus (*Amelanchier* species), berberis (*Berberis* species),

ornamental quince (*Choenomeles* hybrids), dogwood (*Cornus* species) and weigela (*Weigela* hybrids).

Salt. If you have shrubs growing near roads that are strewn with salt every winter, you should choose species that can cope with salt in the soil, such as privet (*Ligustrum vulgare*) or common elder (*Sambucus nigra*).

My tip: Choosing shrubs that can cope well with the conditions in your garden will keep maintenance to a minimum.

The garden and legal matters

Numerous laws and regulations, and sometimes even the lease of a building, will contain rules that the garden owner will have to comply with when planting shrubs and trees. You should be able to obtain information from your local council; they may have a free booklet or brochure dealing with gardening issues.

Boundaries. There are many regulations regarding party walls, hedges and fences. Your council will send you a leaflet about this on request.

Trees and shrubs. If you live in a designated conservation area, all trees are automatically protected and you will have to get prior permission from the council well in advance if you intend to pollard a tree or cut it down completely. In other areas, the council may well apply tree preservation orders to any tree they judge to be of benefit to the public and, once again, permission would be needed to cut the tree in any way.

At present, there are few laws to protect you if a neighbour's trees or shrubs block the light from your garden, but legislation may be coming onto the statute books soon after the number of people who have complained about fast-growing Leylandia hedges.

My tip: Avoid any potential conflict by discussing all shrub planting with your neighbours and asking them to do the same with you. Choose the species with thought: even a tree planted a good distance away may rob your neighbour of light in their living room if it grows very tall and this may cause a conflict years later.

Falling leaves. This is often a cause of a quarrel, but the neighbour will have to put up with it, if it only slightly hampers the use of his garden, is not unusual in the immediate vicinity and cannot be prevented by reasonable means.

Branches and roots. Should either of these grow into or overhang your neighbour's garden, he or she may insist on their removal within a certain specified time, if the use of their garden is impaired. Once the specified time has lapsed the neighbour may, without redress, cut off the branches and roots himself, so long as it is done properly, during the non-growing season. The tree owner has the right to ask for the wood to be returned if he or she wants it.

Fruit. Fruitbearing branches that hang over the boundary into the neighbour's garden can provoke arguments about who may take the fruit. Ornamental shrubs generally only produce inedible fruit that may create quite different problems: if fruit drops onto a public path, the garden owner will be liable should any passersby slip on them.

Fences and walls. The building of fences or walls should always be discussed with your neighbour. In the case of constructions on the boundary, both neighbours are liable for their upkeep.

Tree protection regulations. Check with your council to see if there is a tree preservation order before you do any work on a tree. If you are living in a conservation area, you will have to obtain special permission to cut a tree.

Beautiful but often the subject of disagreements: overhanging branches.

A colourful variety

There is a huge variety of beautiful, flowering ornamental shrubs. You will be spoilt for choice when looking for the species and varieties best suited to your garden.

Preferably choose shrubs that will cope with the soil and climate in your garden. The flowering time will also be important: depending on the species, this may vary from early spring (winter jasmine *Jasminum nudiflorium*) through to autumn (spiraea *Caryopteris x clandonensis*). Clever planting will mean that there is always something flowering in your garden.

Choose the flower colours that you like best. Ornamental shrubs that grow close together and flower at the same time in complementary colours, such as violet (butterfly tree *Buddleia alternifolia*) and orange (Jew's mallow *Kerria japonica*) will look particularly spectacular. A planting of only one colour, like white (spiraea *Spiraea x vanhoutei*) or red (sheep laurel *Kalmia angustifolia*) looks elegant and restrained.

A scented butterfly tree.

Glowing yellow winter jasmine.

An attractive star magnolia.

A graceful bush clover.

Evergreen mountain laurel.

Many ornamental shrubs have scented flowers. In early spring there is witch hazel (*Hamamelis mollis*) with its delicate odour. It is followed by many wonderfully scented species like the star magnolia (*Magnolia stellata*) and roses (*Rosa* species).

Many flowers lure bees and butterflies, like the butterfly tree (*Buddleia davidii*). If you plant these species near a seating area, you will be able to enjoy their scent and watch the creatures attracted by them.

Elegant in shape and colour: the flowers of tho honeysuckle.

The variety of flowering ornamental shrubs is immense

Clematis come in many colours.

The individual hydrangea.

The most beautiful deciduous ornamental shrubs I: from Acer to Jasminum

Name	Colour of flower	Flowering time	Height, in m/yd Growth	Position	Comments
Acer japonicum 'Aureum' Japanese maple	pinkish red with yellow	MSP-LSP	1.5–2.5 bushy	◐	yellow green in summer; golden yellow in autumn
Acer palmatum 'Atropurpureum' red Japanese maple	purple	LSP-ES	2–4 bushy	○-◐	prolific fruits; carmine red autumn colours
Acer palmatum 'Dissectum' purple Japanese maple	purple	LSP-ES	1–3 bushy	○-◐	blackish red, slitted leaves; grows very broad
Amelanchier laevis snowy mespilus	white	MSP-LSP	2–4 bushy	○-◐	red, edible fruit; copes with lime-rich soil
Aralia elata Japanese angelica	creamy white	LS-EA	1 bushy	○-◐	exotic; has thorns; winter protection recommended
Aristolochia macrophylla Dutchman's pipe	yellow green with purple	ES-LS	6–10 climbing	○-●	requires climbing aid and protection from wind; hardiness to pollution
Berberis thunbergii 'Atropurpurea Nana' berberis, dwarf	creamy white to yellow	LSP	0.3–0.6 spherical	○-◐	flowers strongly scented; thorns on shoots; berries
Buddleia davidii hybrids butterfly tree	white, pink, red, lilac	MS-MA	2–3 bushy	○	scented; after flowering, shorten by a third
Callicarpa bodinieri 'Profusion' beauty berry	lilac pink	MS-LS	1 bushy	○	dark brown shoots; violet berries
Calycanthus floridus	brown to dark red	ES-MS	2–3 bushy	○	flowers, leaves and bark strongly scented
Caryopteris x clandonensis blue spiraea	sky blue to dark blue	LS-EA	1 bushy	○	requires winter protection; cut back in spring
Ceanothus hybrids Californian lilac	light to dark blue	MS-MA	1 bushy	○	requires winter protection; cut back in spring
Cercis siliquastrum Judas tree	purple pink to violet	MSP-LSP	3–5 tree	○	protected position; forms red pods
Chimonanthus praecox winter sweet	yellow with brown red	EW-ESP	2–3 bushy	○	for wine-growing climate; also for espalier; strongly scented
Chionanthus virginicus fringe tree	white	ES	3–5 bushy	○	slightly acid soils; light yellow autumn colours
Chaenomeles japonica japonica or Japanese quince	orange to brick red	LW-MSP	0.8–1.5 bushy	○	fairly undemanding; edible quinces
Clematis species/ – hybrids clematis	white, yellow, pinkish red, lilac	LSP-EA	2–6 climbing	◐-◐	many species and varieties; some require cutting
Cornus alba 'Elegantissima' dogwood, red-barked	yellowish white	LSP-ES	2–3 bushy	○-◐	variegated leaves; carmine red in autumn
Cornus canadensis dogwood	whitish pink	ES-MS	0.1–0.2 creeping	○-◐	acid soil; red berries; ground-covering
Cornus florida dogwood	white to pinkish red	LSP-ES	4–6 bushy	○	sensitive to lime; red autumn colouring
Cornus kousa Japanese dogwood	white with pink	LSP-ES	5–7 bushy	○-◐	sensitive to lime; pinkish red fruit
Cornus mas Cornelian cherry	greenish yellow	ESP-MSP	4–5 bushy	○-●	edible red fruit; can cope with cutting
Corylopsis pauciflora winter hazel	delicate yellow	ESP-MSP	1–2 bushy	○-◐	protect from late frosts; do not cut back

 = sunny   = semi-shade   = shade   = toxic   ESP = early Spring, MSP = mid-Spring, LSP = late Spring; ES = early Summer, MS = mid-Summer

The most beautiful deciduous ornamental shrubs I: from Acer to Jasminum

Name		Colour of flower	Flowering time	Height, in m/yd Growth	Position	Comments
Corylus avellana 'Contorta' corkscrew hazel		greenish yellow	LW–ESP	2–2.5 bushy	○-●	conspicuous growth; attractive as solitary
Corylus maxima 'Purpurea' purple-leaved filbert		reddish green	LW–ESP	3–4 bushy	○-◐	black red foliage; reddish brown, edible nuts
Cotinus coggygria 'Royal Purple', smoke bush	☠	greenish red	ES–MS	2–3 bushy	○-◐	black red foliage; red silvery fruit stands
Crataegus laevigata 'Paul's Scarlet', hawthorn		red	LSP–ES	3–5 tree	○	red fruit; particularly attractive as solitary
Cytisus x praecox broom		white, yellow, pink, red	MSP–LSP	1–1.5 bushy	○-◐	scented; hangs over; cut back
Deutzia gracilis deutzia		white	LSP–ES	0.5–1 bushy	○-◐	undemanding; profusely flowering; cut back
Elsholtzia stauntonii		purple to carmine pink	EA–MA	1 bushy	○	semi-bush; protected position and winter protection
Erica carnea winter heather		pink, red, violet	EW–LW	0.3 cushion-like	○	manages with lime; hardy to pollution; needs cutting back
Euonymus planipes common spindle	☠	yellow green	LSP–ES	3–5 bushy	○-●	red orange fruit; carmine red autumn colours
Exochorda racemosa pearl bush		brilliant white	LSP	3–4 bushy	○	undemanding; flowers profusely and scented
Forsythia x intermedia forsythia		light to golden yellow	MSP–LSP	2–4 bushy	○-◐	undemanding; requires regular cutting back
Fothergilla gardenii fothergilla		yellowish white	MSP–LSP	0.5–1 bushy	○-◐	undemanding; hangs very wide when older
Gaultheria procumbens partridgeberry		white to light pink	ES–LS	0.3 creeping	○-◐	scarlet berries; good ground-covering
Hamamelis japonica Japanese witch hazel		yellow	LW–MSP	2–3 bushy	○-◐	funnel-shaped crown; orange red autumn colours
Hamamelis mollis witch hazel		golden yellow with red	MW–ESP	2–5 bushy	○-◐	undemanding; scented; golden yellow autumn colours
Hibiscus syriacus tree hollyhock		white, pink, red, lilac	MS–EA	1–2 bushy	○	many varieties; requires protected position
Hydrangea anomala ssp. petiolaris hydrangea or hortensia		white	ES–MS	5–7 climbing	◐-●	no climbing aid needed; scented; yellow autumn colour
Hydrangea arborescens hydrangea		creamy white	MS–EA	2–3 bushy	○-●	many varieties; profusely flowering; yellow autumn colour
Hydrangea aspera ssp. argentiana hydrangea		violet with white	MS–LS	2 bushy	○	no lime; velvety leaves; spreads slowly
Hydrangea hybrids garden hydrangea		white, pink, purple, blue	MS–EA	1–2 bushy	○-◐	slightly acid soil; cut back regularly
Hydrangea paniculata garden hydrangea		creamy white to pink	MS–LS	2–3 bushy	◐-●	many varieties; no lime; does not mind cutting back
Hypericum x moserianum St. John's wort		golden yellow	ES–MA	0.3–0.5 bushy	○-◐	undemanding; filler bush and ground-covering
Jasminum nudiflorum winter jasmine		yellow	EW–ESP	1–3 bushy	○-◐	loves lime; overhanging; suitable for espalier

LS = late Summer; EA = early Autumn, MA = mid- Autumn, LA late Autumn; EW = early Winter, MW = mid-Winter, LW = late Winter

A colourful variety

While some ornamental shrubs are still unfolding their beautiful flowers, others are already busy forming the first berries. The colourful splendour of fruits reaches a climax in the autumn and in some species, like cotoneaster (*Cotoneaster dammeri*), the berries still decorate its branches well into the winter. Some fruits are, however, toxic. If you have small children or pets in your household, it might be better to leave out these species and choose non-toxic ones instead.

The leaves of many ornamental shrubs also ensure a wealth of colours in the autumn, like maple (*Acer palmatum*) and dogwood (*Cornus* species). They will produce a veritable firework display of colour in glowing shades of yellow and red, right through to wine purple. Cleverly arranged in small groups, they can look stunning. Some of them even display colourful new growth in the spring, such as andromeda (*Pieris japonica*) or golden maple (*Acer japonicum* 'Aureum').

Rowan leaves covered in frost.

Tasty snowy mespilus berries.

Extravagant rosehips.

Ornamental apples.

Delicate berberis berries.

Some fruits of ornamental shrubs are rich in vitamins and are edible uncooked, such as the fruit of the snowy mespilus (*Amelanchier laevis*). Other fruits can be eaten after cooking them, such as rosehips (*Rosa* species), apples or rowan berries (*Sorbus aucuparia*). However, others are not edible by humans, and may even be toxic, but serve as food for birds, such as ornamental apple species (*Malus* species) or the berries of mahonia (*Mahonia aquifolium*). Trees and bushes also offer possible nest sites for birds.

Conspicuous but toxic: the fruit of the spindle berry tree.

Colourful splendour that often lasts a long time: leaves and fruits of ornamental shrubs

Mahonia fruit with blueish bloom.

Exotic flowering dogwood.

The most beautiful deciduous ornamental shrubs II: from Kolkwitzia to Weigela

Name		Colour of flower	Flowering time	Height, in m/yd Growth	Position	Comments
Kolkwitzia amabilis beauty bush		light pink	LSP–ES	2–3 bushy	○ - ◐	copes with lime; profusely flowering
Lespedeza thunbergii bush clover		pink to violet red	LS–EA	1–2 bushy	○	requires protected position; grows overhanging
Lonicera species honeysuckle	☠	white, yellow, orange, red	LSP–LS	3–6 bushy	○ - ●	also climbing species; red/black berries
Magnolia x soulangiana magnolia		whitish pink	MSP–LSP	4–5 tree	○	sheltered position; no lime; many hybrids
Magnolia stellata star magnolia		white	ESP–MSP	2–3 bushy	○ - ◐	sheltered position; no lime; no cutting back
Malus floribunda ornamental apple		white, pink, red, lilac	LSP	3–5 tree	○ - ◐	many varieties; copes with lime; best as solitary
Paeonia suffruticosa mountain peony		white, yellow, pink, red, lilac	LSP–ES	0.8–1 bushy	○ - ◐	sheltered position; many varieties/hybrids
Perovskia atriplicifolia Russian sage		violet blue	LS–EA	1 bushy	○	sheltered position; cut back regularly
Prunus cerasifera 'Nigra' prunus		pinkish red	MSP–LSP	4–6 tree	○	undemanding; hardy to pollution; leaves blackish red
Prunus triloba almond		pink	ESP–MSP	1–2 bushy	○	copes with lime; best as solitary
Ribes sanguineum flowering currant		dark red	MSP–LSP	1.5–2 bushy	○ - ◐	undemanding; scented; edible, black berries
Rosa species/ varieties roses		white, yellow, pink, red, lilac	LSP–MA	0.2–4 bushy	○	flowers once/often; scented; also climbing
Spiraea x arguta bridal wreath		white	MSP–LSP	1.5–2.5 bushy	○ - ◐	undemanding; scented; overhanging shoots
Syringa x persica lilac		purplish lilac	MSP–LSP	1–2 bushy	○ - ◐	undemanding; dainty, overhanging growth
Syringa reflexa lilac		dark pink to red	ES–MS	2–4 bushy	○ - ◐	intensely scented; overhanging growth
Syringa vulgaris hybrids common lilac		white, yellow, pink, red, lilac	LSP–ES	4–6 bushy	○ - ◐	many varieties; often scented; solitary or in groups
Tamarix ramosissima tamarisk		pink	MS–EA	3–4 bushy	○	copes with dryness; best as a solitary
Viburnum x burkwoodii snowball		pink to white	ESP–MSP	2–3 bushy	○ - ◐	strongly scented; evergreen in mild winters
Viburnum carlesii Korean snowball		pink to white	MSP–LSP	1–1.5 bushy	○ - ◐	beguiling scent; best as a solitary
Viburnum farreri snowball, scented		white to pink	LA–ESP	2–3 bushy	○ - ◐	beguiling scent; grows stiffly upright
Viburnum opulus 'Compactum' common snowball	☠	creamy white	LSP–ES	1 bushy	○ - ◐	remains small; also suitable for rockeries and trough gardens
Weigela florida 'Purpurea' weigela, dwarf		dark pink	LSP–ES	1 bushy	○ - ◐	brownish red leaves; also as a solitary
Weigela hybrids weigela		white, pink, red	LSP–MS	2–3 bushy	○ - ◐	undemanding; many varieties; thin out often

 = sunny  = semi-shade = shade = toxic

The most beautiful evergreen deciduous and coniferous shrubs

Name		Colour of foliage/needes	Growth	Height, in m/yd	Position	Comments
Abies koreana fir		dark to blue green	conical	4–5	○-◐	slow growing; violet cones
Buxus sempervirens box	☠	dark to blue green	conical to egg-shaped	0.8–2	○-●	slow growing; can take cutting back
Buxus sempervirens 'Marginata' box		green, yellow seam	conical	2	○-◐	interesting variegated variety
Cedrus deodara 'Golden Horizon' dwarf himalayan cedar		yellow to greenish yellow	wide and flat	0.7	○	no lime; red cones; best as solitary
Chamaecyparis pisifera Sawara cypress		yellow green, grey green, blue green	conical to sherical	1–5	○-◐	many varieties; small, brown, conical cones
Cotoneaster dammeri cotoneaster		dark green shiny	creeping	0.2–1	○-◐	white flowers; red berries; good ground-covering
Euonymus fortunei spindle		light to dark green	creeping	0.2–0.6	○-●	many varieties; also variegated; good ground covering
Hedera helix ivy	☠	dark green, yellow variegated	climbing; bushy	5–10	◐-●	no climbing aid needed; black, toxic berries
Ilex aquifolium holly	☠	dark green, yellow variegated	broad-conical	4–5	◐-●	many varieties; red, toxic berries; male and female flowers
Juniperus communis juniper		grey green to blue green	conical to pillar-shaped	1–3	○-◐	many varieties; strongly flavoured, edible, black berries
Kalmia latifolia mountain laurel	☠	dark green, red new growth	broad and upright	1	●	no lime; pink flowers; also variegated varieties
Mahonia aquifolium mahonia Oregon grape	☠	dark green, denticulate	upright; arching	0.8–1.5	○-◐	yellow flower, scented; bluish black berries
Mahonia bealei mahonia	☠	dark green, denticulate	upright; spiky	1.5–2	●	sheltered position; light yellow flower, scented
Picea breweriana spruce		blue green to dark green	broadly conical	5–7	○-◐	no lime; undemanding; violet brown cones
Pieris japonica andromeda	☠	matt green to dark green	open; hanging	2–3	●	acid, moist soil; white/pink flowers
Pinus mugo mountain pine		blue green to dark green	broadly bushy	0.5–5	○	many varieties; also on lime; brown cones
Rhododendron hybrids rhododendron	☠	dark green to silver green	broadly bushy	0.5–1	●	acid soil; position sheltered from wind; groups
Skimmia japonica skimmia		strong to yellow green	broadly conical	0.5–1	●	brownish red flower; red fruit; can cope with lime
Taxus baccata yew	☠	dark green to blue green	broad to pillar-shaped	0.6–4	◐-●	many varieties with differing growth; red berries
Thuja occidentalis 'Emerald' white cedar	☠	strong green	broadly conical	2.5–6	○-◐	also on lime; copes with cutting back; many varieties
Tsuga canadensis 'Nana Gracilis' dwarf eastern hemlock		light green to dark green	broadly conical	0.5	●	position sheltered from wind; do not cut back
Vinca minor lesser periwinkle		strong green	creeping	0.15	◐-●	light blue flowers; good ground-covering

Ideas, tips and tricks

Perfect design

The possibilities for utilizing ornamental shrubs and trees in your garden are endless. Planting does need to be thought through carefully, however. The following pages will equip you with all the important basics of design and some examples for any area of the garden.

Top: Clematis – here a 'Vivian Penell' – are among the most beautiful climbing shrubs.
Left: Even small garden spaces can be designed in a variety of ways by using ornamental shrubs.

Perfect design

Planning your garden

It makes no difference whether you want to redesign an existing garden or transform a bare plot into a 'green oasis'. Everything should be thoroughly planned beforehand. Proceed as follows, in order to avoid making mistakes that can take a great deal of time, effort and money to correct:
● Take your time and inspect the plot in peace, collecting ideas and deciding your preferences.
● Draw a scale sketch of the garden.
● Mark in all existing shrubs and trees, even those that grow on your neighbours' plots but can be seen from your garden and cast shadows.
● When planning, consider that the new design should complement your house and fit into the surroundings.
● Incorporate the surroundings into your garden design, by framing an attractive view with shrubs and trees.
● Ugly spots can be hidden from view by covering them up with shrubs and trees.
● Try to divide up the garden in as many varied areas as possible, to make it look larger and more interesting.
● Remember that a garden needs plenty of sun and should not be shaded too much by shrubs and trees.
● Find out about any legal matters long before you proceed to planting (see page 10).

Shapes of growth

Shrubs and trees are effective all year round, due to their growth and their contours. Obtain all the necessary information on characteristics of growth from good tree nursery catalogues well beforehand, and remember to anticipate how shrubs and trees will look when they have no leaves on them. You will be able to create interesting contrasts and tension by combining different shapes of growth. By choosing similar shapes of growth, you will, on the other hand, create peaceful, harmonious areas.

Leaves
It is possible to forget that even the leaves will influence the effect of the shrub: large areas of foliage make the shrub appear luxuriant. Filigree leaves, on the other hand, give it a light, delicate appearance. Plants with large leaves are usually suitable on their own and mainly for larger gardens. In a small garden, preferably choose shrubs with more delicate foliage, or the shrub will seem overladen. Combining different shapes and colours of leaves will also result in interesting contrasts.

Colours

Choose the colours according to your own preferences, but consider the following basic rules:
● Complementary colours like blue and yellow, red and green, orange and lilac have a particularly bright and lively effect.
● Colour trios like yellow-red-blue will appear very stark or even shrill. Pastel colours (colours lightened with white) create a much quieter impression.
● White and green will tone down strong contrasts.
● Colour combinations such as yellow, ochre and orange give an elegant touch.
● Combinations of one colour in several different shades, from light to dark, will also create an elegant, peaceful look.
● Too many colours in a small space rarely look good.
● Consider the flowering times of the shrubs and trees: you can achieve different colour combinations at different times of the year.
My tip: Small gardens will appear larger if only a few colours and hardly any contrasts are used. Preferably choose combinations of related or pastel colours. Tones of blue in the background enlarge the garden visually, especially if you have warm yellow and red shades in the foreground.

The little tree with its compact, spherical crown is a real eye-catcher in this herbaceous border. The delicate foliage fits well into the whole plantation and displays the flowers to best advantage. Even in winter, the evergreen species will provide an attractive sight in the bed.

Practise: basic rules of design

Here you will find some typical examples of the use of ornamental shrubs and trees in a garden; they are discussed in more depth in the following pages.

Garden example
Illustration 1

The art of designing a garden consists of framing it attractively with the help of shrubs and trees and dividing it up sensibly and with variety. Observe the following basic rules:
● Tall shrubs and trees should be placed near the edges.
● Stagger the heights, in order to create tension.
● Employ conifers sparingly, as they tend to have a gloomy effect.

Seating area
Illustration 1a

A seating area in your garden is an ideal place to relax, especially in the summer, when it can get very hot on the patio. Here, a single tree dispenses pleasant shade and the pond supplies an additional cooling feature. Other types of grouped shrubs or a bower can frame a seating area.

The edge of a pond
Illustration 1b

A pond should be framed by planting along its edges; without plants, it can look like an alien feature. For this purpose choose species with shoots that hang down attractively over the water's edge. Graduate the plants towards the garden itself and end up with low-growing ornamental shrubs that you can combine with herbaceous plants.

Patio
Illustration 1c

Here too, shrubs have been employed as

*1a A **garden seat** in the pleasant shade of ornamental shrubs offers relaxation and peace.*

*1b The **pond** is linked visually with the rest of the garden when overhanging ornamental shrubs are planted round the edges.*

indispensable shade providers – whether on an espalier, as a tree close to the house or as a group – and they will protect you from the gaze of passersby. Pay particular attention to the beauty of the flowers and their scents. In order to make this little garden appear larger, the seating area was installed on a slightly lower level. A wall of earth was heaped up towards the path and planted with semi-tall shrubs and trees.

Mixed borders
Illustration 1d

Many ornamental shrubs go well with herbaceous plants. You can combine their different shapes of growth to create interesting groups (see photo, page 38). Preferably pick asymmetrical combinations.

The shrubs should not dominate too much. Choose the colours of the flowers according to the colour design rules (see page 22).

1 Several typical situations in a garden.

1c The patio is shielded by shrubs.

1d Mixed borders with shrubs and herb plants.

Periwinkles make good neutral accompanying plants, and they will also provide a calm background for lively mixtures of colours.

Views
Illustration 1e

Try and create a frame around a particularly attractive view into the surrounding landscape by placing ornamental shrubs and trees strategically, making sure you do not inadvertently close off the view. This will also create a connection between the garden and its surroundings and the space will be visually enlarged, while the private area of your garden is still effectively delimited. Taller evergreens are particularly suited to this purpose, as they will continue to provide colour even in the winter months.

Areas divided off
Illustration 1f

Vegetable patches and compost heaps are often not so attractive. Cover them with the help of a group of shrubs or trees that will not, however, cast too much shade on the

1e A view through a framework of shrubs and trees.

1f Areas can be decoratively partitioned off with the help of shrubs and trees.

vegetable patches. You may decorate the entrance with an arch. Once you have stepped through it, you can get an overview of this little area. A group of dustbins or a small seating area could also be hidden in this way.

Solitary shrubs and trees

By 'solitaries', we mean trees or shrubs that are standing on their own. No neighbouring plants are meant to detract from their beauty. A solitary is often placed in the centre of a lawn. Nearer to the house, it will play the role of a shade-dispensing tree. But a solitary may also create a feature in a bed or border.

Tree nursery catalogues will often use the term 'solitary'. Here, it means that the shrub or tree was transplanted at least three times during its growth. It will be relatively large and will provide an eye-catching feature in your garden immediately after planting. Shrubs and trees that have been grown without so much time and effort will be cheaper, but they will need time to give character to your garden.

Characteristic features. Solitary shrubs or trees should fulfil as many of the following qualities as possible:
● an interesting shape of growth – overhanging, umbrella-like, pillar-shaped or just bizarre;
● it should have beautiful flowers, preferably scented ones;
● it should have an interesting flower shape and colours;
● it should have brilliantly coloured fruits and intense autumn colouring;
● it should have an interesting bark structure and colour.

Important: before buying anything, find out what size your chosen species is likely to attain.

It should still be a good distance from other shrubs and trees, even after many years, and should not appear oppressive if it stands close to the house. Choose a deciduous tree for planting close to the house, so that sunlight can penetrate the living room in winter months.

Deciduous trees that are suitable as solitaries:
● Japanese maple (*Acer japonicum*, many varieties), beautiful autumn colouring, 2–4m (6–13ft)
● Maple (*Acer negundo* 'Variegatum'), white-edged leaves, 5–7m (16–23ft)
● Fan maple (*Acer palmatum*, many varieties), also with all-year coloured foliage, 1–3m (3–9ft)
● Weeping birch (*Betula pendula* 'Youngii'), umbrella-shaped crown, hanging branches, 4–6m (13–20ft)
● Japanese flowering cherry (*Prunus serrulata*, many varieties) with pink to white, often scented flowers, conspicuous bark and pillar-shaped to hanging growth, 3–6m (9–20ft)
● Oak (*Quercus ilicifolia*), spiky bush, yellowish red autumn foliage, 4–6m (13–20ft)
● Locust tree (*Robinia pseudoacacia* 'Umbraculifera'), scented, white flowers, spherical crown, 3–4m (9–13ft)
● Rowan (*Sorbus aucuparia* 'Fastigiata'), narrowish, cone-shaped growth, white flowers, dark red berries, yellow-orange autumnal colouring
● Rowan (*Sorbus vilmorinii*), pink flowers, hanging side

shoots, pink berries, orange-red autumnal colouring, 3–6m (9–20ft)

Conifers that are suitable as solitaries:
● Korean fir (*Abies koreana*), grows cone-shaped, violet brown cones, 5–7m (16–23ft)
● Lawson cypress (*Chamaecyparis lawsoniana*, many varieties), 2–7m (6–23ft)
● Juniper (*Juniperus chinensis*, many varieties), 2–7m (6–23ft)
● Spruce (*Picea glauca* 'Conica'), grows in a cone shape, 2–3m (6–9ft)
● Pine (*Pinus parviflora*), small crown, decorative, 5–10m (16–32ft)
● Yew (*Taxus bacata* 'Fastigiata'), narrow column, 3–5m (9–16ft)
● Cedar (*Thuja occidentalis* 'Emerald'), intensely green, 4–6m (13–20ft)

Note: The tables on pages 14–15 and 18–19 list further species that are suitable as solitaries.

Groups of shrubs and trees

A group of shrubs and trees consists, as a rule, of one or two taller shrubs and three to six lower bushes of varying heights. Choose slower-growing or sparse shrubs for very small gardens. Consider the following when making your choice:
● Species that you combine must have similar demands with respect to position.

A group of different varieties of dogwood.

● Use your own taste in combining species with different flowering times or those that burst into a firework display of colour all at the same time. In the latter case, match the colours according to the basic rules (see page 22).

● Do not just choose conspicuously magnificent shrubs. Plainer surrounding plants will enhance the beauty of more conspicuous ones.

● There are so many different species and varieties of some shrubs that you will be able to create a varied group even by sticking to a selection from one species, for example, with dogwood (*Cornus*, see photo left) or rhododendron (*Rhododendron*, see photo page 31).

● Conifers that do not grow too tall may provide the centre for a mixed group of deciduous trees. They create a darker background, in front of which flowering shrubs will look particularly effective.

A clever choice of shrubs will mean your group will delight you all year round with its cycle of colour highlights.

● Taller shrubs will cast shadows. Use suitably tolerant neighbouring shrubs.

● Space plants carefully so that the crowns of the fully grown shrubs only overlap in the outermost quarters.

● The group will have a dramatic tension if you combine pillar-shaped types with spherical and broadly spreading shapes of growth.

● Play a little with varying shapes and colours of leaves. Do not, however, choose more than one variegated variety, or the whole group will look too restless.

Perfect design

Patios

You will want to enjoy a view from your patio out into the garden. If possible, do not block it with tall shrubs. An edge planting will make the patio comfortable and inviting. Borders or small groups of cushion-shaped herbaceous plants (see accompanying plants, page 38) and low-growing bushes (see tables, pages 14–15 and 18–19) will create a gentle transition to the lawn and garden. Choose shrubs with beautiful, scented flowers, so that you can enjoy them when sitting on the patio.

If you plant smaller, evergreen shrubs and early spring flowering species like witch hazel (*Hamamelis* species and varieties), you will have a pleasant view even in the winter, looking out of the window onto the patio.

A visual screen. Do you feel as though you are on display sitting on your patio? There is sure to be a 'plant' to cure that. First, try looking into your garden from the outside and note the points at which you can be overlooked. If it is only a small area, you can:
● Plant an appropriate large bush in a strategic position.
● Close a gap by planting a dwarf climbing plant in a trough, that can be moved, or on an espalier.

If, however, most of the patio can be overlooked, you could:
● Plant a hedge along the boundary of your plot (see page 30).
● Surround your patio with climbing plants grown on espaliers, or with a visual screen of these plants. A pergola covered with green climbing plants will also provide protection against onlookers from above and from too much sun.
● Place the seating area on a lower (sunken) level (see page 25).

Seating areas in your garden

It can become unbearably hot on the patio in summer. A seat in the shade of ornamental shrubs, somewhere in the garden, will be ideal. In the simplest case, take a deckchair or lounger and go off into the bushes, but it is much more pleasant to create a permanent seat where you have an attractive view. First, think about what you want to do in this position: be alone, read, rest or sit with others in a pleasant social gathering? This will determine the size of the seating area. The bench or group of seats should match the style of your garden. The more natural the planning around it, the more natural the materials should be, such as wood or stone (see photo, page 29, centre and bottom left).

For a more permanent seat, it is best to create a firm base using gravel or, better still, paving slabs or stones. With respect to shrubs and trees, you have the following options:
● A seat or bench under a tree is sheltered and shaded by it. In the case of a deciduous tree, you will be able to enjoy weaker sunlight there in spring and autumn. If you build a pond near the seating area, this will also help to cool the air. The choice of the height of the tree will be determined by the size of the garden (see photos, page 29, top left and centre right).
● A bower or pergola – perhaps with climbing roses (see photo, page 29, centre left) – will also shelter the seating area and they require less space.
● Groups of shrubs surrounding the bench will provide shade, a visual screen and will also be pleasant to look at and smell during the flowering season.
● Dense cut hedges provide shelter from draughts. You could even create a backrest out of shaped, evergreen shrubs (see photo, page 29, top right).

English elegance with a well cared for lawn

Hedge cut in the shape of a seat.

Surrounded by wonderful scent.

A place for working in peace.

A shady spot for a rest.

A little corner close to nature.

A multitude of seating arrangements

These are places for relaxing and contemplation on your own, or for a gathering with family and friends. The benches are made of elegant or plain materials, freshly painted or aged gracefully, depending on the taste of the user.

Perfect design

Hedges

Where houses are built very close together and gardens are overlooked, hedges have an important function: they will delimit the garden like a living wall, providing a screen against prying eyes, noise and wind. They may cover up ugly views. Birds, insects and other small creatures will find nourishment, nesting spaces and cover in them. Consider the following in the planning stage:
● Before planting, obtain information on growth, spacing of plants and the final size of the shrubs concerned.
● If the hedge is intended as shelter against wind, it needs to stand at right angles to the usual direction of the wind and be densely planted.
● Leaves will absorb noise better than conifer needles. Evergreen deciduous shrubs are most suitable for protection against noise. The effect is greater if you plant the hedge on top of a soundproof wall (see page 24).
● Evergreen hedges provide shelter all year round.
● Hedges of deciduous shrubs will become transparent in winter, but will also let more light and sunlight into the garden.
● Windows, patios and the kitchen garden should not be overshadowed by hedges.
● Hedges that require cutting (see below) are more labour-intensive than free-growing ones, but they require less room.

● The smaller the garden, the more dainty the hedge should be.
● Hedges will often be too overpowering for very small gardens. Allow climbing shrubs to grow up a fence for a space-saving alternative.
● Keep to the minimum distance from the boundary when planting, or discuss the matter with your neighbour. A communal hedge on the boundary will save both money and space.

Types and variations

Varied hedges can be designed even in the smallest gardens:
Cut hedge: these consist of just one species of plant, a deciduous or coniferous shrub that does not mind being cut, that may be evergreen or may lose its leaves. It will have to be cut at least once a year (see page 48). Of all kinds of hedges, it will require the least amount of space. The narrowest hedges are formed by yew (*Taxus baccata*), that can be cut back to a width of only 30cm (12in). Long cut hedges will often appear very uniform and boring. Short ones or tall ones, on the other hand, may create boundaries for certain parts of the garden, and low ones may serve as a border edging (see page 32).
● Coniferous shrubs that cope with cutting back, besides the yew, are blue Lawson cypress

(*Chamaecyparis lawsoniana* 'Alumnii') and the cone-shaped cedar (*Thuja occidentalis* 'Holmstrup').
● Evergreen deciduous shrubs that do not mind cutting are the large-leafed berberis (*Berberis julianae*), the tall box (*Buxus sempervirens* 'Rotundifolia'), the mountain holly (*Ilex crenata* 'Convexa'), the hedge honeysuckle (*Lonicera nitida* 'Elegant'), mahonia (*Mahonia aquifolium*), hedge cherry (*Prunus laurocerasus* 'Herbergii') and firethorn (*Pyracantha coccinea* 'Red Column').
● Shrubs that lose their leaves and cope with cutting are the green hedge berberis (*Berberis thunbergii*), the hornbeam (*Carpinus betulus*), red dogwood (*Cornus sanguinea*), rock cotoneaster (*Cotoneaster praecox*) and forsythia (*Forsythia x intermedia*).
Free-growing hedges. You can mix different species. The hedge should not be cut, but depending on the species, a lot of leaves will fall off in the autumn. Such a hedge will, however, take up a width of 2 to 3m (6 to 9ft).
● Wild hedges can be assembled out of indigenous shrubs: wild roses (*Rosa rubiginosa* and *R. rugosa*), spindle tree (*Euonymus europaea*), hedge honeysuckle (*Lonicera xylosteum*), sloe or blackthorn (*Prunus spinosa*) and elder (*Sambucus nigra*). They are undemanding and ecologically

A hedge made of flowering dogwood, rhododendron and kolkwitzia.

valuable, but often do not produce many flowers.

● Flowering hedges can consist of profusely flowering varieties: flowering dogwood (*Cornus florida*, white and pink, see photo above), Deutzia roses (*Deutzia x hybrida* 'Mont Rose', pink), beauty bush (*Kolkwitzia amabilis*, pink), bridal wreath (*Spiraea x* 'Arguta', white), lilac (*Syringa vulgaris*, white, yellow, pink, red, lilac, and blue), large-flowered snowball (*Viburnum x carlcephalum*, white) and weigela (*Weigela* hybrids, pink and red).

● If you choose to place evergreen shrubs such as yew (*Taxus x media* 'Hicksii'), large-leafed berberis (*Berberis julianae*) or holly (*Ilex aquifolium*) between the hedges, then this will help to loosen up the whole.

Perfect design

Formal gardens

Formal gardens feature symmetrically planted shrubs cut into geometric shapes to form the basic framework. With their simple, clear structures, these designs are particularly suitable for small gardens and also for long, narrow plots of ground that can be optically widened by creating divisions running at right angles. The cost of creating such a garden, however, and the amount of effort required to look after it are relatively high. Classical formal gardens have the following characteristics:
● They are bordered by a trimmed hedge, usually evergreen.
● The garden will be divided within itself by trimmed hedges or espaliers.
● Borders and paths will be framed by low borders of shrubs cut in geometrical patterns.
● The beds themselves are often divided up again ornamentally by low-growing, cut shrubs.
● Other features include standard trees cut into unusual shapes, walkways, fountains, sculptures, benches and bowers.
● Lawns, if present at all, occur only in a very short-cut form.
● Paved areas and/or gravel emphasize the severity of this type of garden.
● Luxuriantly planted beds with herbs or flowers can soften the severity of the geometric shapes.
● Colours tend to be restrained, often just various shades of green creating delicate accents.
● The edged paths create visual axes that make small gardens appear larger.

Edging shrubs

Not all shrubs that can be cut can also be made to grow low. *Edging up to 45cm (18in) tall* can be formed with any of the following:
● The evergreen edging box (*Buxus sempervirens* 'Suffruticosa'; see photos, right) is the most popular species for this purpose, grows slowly and is easy to propagate from cuttings (see page 42).
● Lavender (*Lavandula angustifolia* 'Hidecote') possesses pleasing, scented evergreen and grey-green leaves. It flowers in high summer with blue violet spikes and is easy to propagate.
● *Teucrium chamaedrys* is a deep green, evergreen semi-bush. It is strongly scented and forms small, pink flower spikes in high summer. In regions with a cold climate it may die back in freezing weather, but will generally produce new growth again in the spring.
● Lavender cotton (*Santolina chamaecyparissus*) is also an evergreen semi-bush but has grey, felty, feathery leaves. In high summer, it forms small, yellow flowerheads. It requires a sheltered position and should be covered up with conifer branches in winter.
Edging from 50–90cm (20–35in) tall can be created with any of the following:
● Privet (*Ligustrum ovalifolium*) that remains evergreen in mild climates and forms white, strongly scented flower racemes in the first month of summer.
● The evergreen yew (*Taxus baccata*).
Important: If you want to enjoy flowers, delay cutting the edging until late summer.

The following species, beside box, yew and privet, are suitable for cutting into shapes. All are evergreen and shiny dark green:
● Holly (*Ilex quifolium*),
● Cedar (*Thuja occidentalis* 'Ellwangeriana'),
● Cherry laurel (*Prunus laurocerasus* 'Reynvaanii').

Geometric shapes

The special effect of a formal garden is created by its symmetry.
● The beds can be enclosed in a variety of different geometric shapes: rectangle (see photo, top right), square, diamond, triangle, circle (see photo, bottom right), a semi-circle or quarter circle, an oval or combinations of rectangles and segments of circles.
● Within a bed, there are a whole host of further sub-divisions: crosses, diagonals, turning a motif through a 90 degree angle, for example, or by fitting circles into squares.

The most involved shapes can be found in intricate English knot gardens, where curving bands of low shrubs in different shades of green appear to cross over each other in the most complicated patterns.

● The intersection of two paths can be a simple crosspath (see photo, top right), but it is often widened to form a roundel. In the centre, a fountain, a solitary tree, a sculpture, or a sun dial (see photo, bottom right) will create emphases.

My tip: If a formal garden is too complicated for you, why not just extract one element from it, like box trees cut in a spherical shape. They harmonize well with herbaceous plants, and in the winter, when the latter have faded, the stark, graphic shapes of these globes will dominate the scene.

Framed and severely rectangular.

A playful design of a double circle and box spheres.

Ivy tendrils wind romantically around a fence and gateway.

Rose and honeysuckle.

A natural garden

A garden that is created in harmony with nature has its very own aesthetic charm. Choose indigenous plants that would thrive well in this location anyway.

Wild hedges (see page 30) are appropriate for creating **boundaries**, or simple wooden fences. These look even more natural if they are covered in green climbing plants. For example, ivy (*Hedera helix*, see photo above, evergreen), honeysuckle (*Lonicera caprifolium* or *Lonicera periclymenum*, see photo left) or spring-flowering clematis (*Clematis alpina*).

A multitude of species. If you plant as many indigenous species as possible, you will create living space for a large number of birds, insects and small creatures.

Here are some further shrubs for small groups or solitaries (height 2–5m/6–15ft):
snowy mespilus (*Amelanchier laevis*, see photo, page 16) and buckthorn (*Hippophae rhamnoides*), both with edible fruit; common privet (*Ligustrum vulgare*), with its toxic, blueish-black berries; willow (*Salix cinerea*); elder (*Sambucus racemosa*) and common snowball (*Viburnum opulus*), both with red berries.

The heather garden

This is counted as a type of natural garden: its great model is the heathland of the Lüneburger Heide in Germany, and it is characterized by heathers and junipers. The following are important for this type of garden:
● A poor, acid, sandy or peaty soil.
● A heather garden will only really work if a larger area is covered in plants. If possible, plant cushions of 20–30 plants per variety.
● The work done by the heathland sheep in a natural setting will have to be carried out by you, the gardener: cutting back the plants regularly, so they do not stop flowering. In the case of spring and summer flowering species, this should be done after flowering. In the case of autumn and winter flowering

species and varieties, cut them back in the spring.
Heathers. There are a number of evergreen species. They are dwarf bushes and will flower at varying times:
● Common heather (*Calluna vulgaris*), many varieties, flowers from the second month of summer through to the middle of the autumn, white, pink, red, lilac, and violet.
● Irish heath (*Daboecia cantabrica*), a few varieties, flowers from early summer to early autumn, white, pink, purple and violet. Will need winter protection in some regions with a cold climate.
● Winter heather (*Erica carnea*), many varieties, flowers from early winter to late spring, white, pink, red and violet. It is the only species that will also cope with chalky soil or lime.
My tip: Use different varieties of winter heather to design a heather garden on chalky soil.
Accompanying shrubs.
Evergreen shrubs like juniper (*Juniperus communis*) and mountain pine (*Pinus mugo*) will create a dark green background for the flowering tufts of heather. The community of heathland plants also includes the dwarf birch (*Betula nana*), broom (*Cytisus scoparius*) with yolk-yellow coloured flowers from late spring to early summer, and broom (*Genista tinctoria*) with yellow flowers from mid to late summer.

A natural pond

There should always be water in a natural garden. A garden from a size of 500sq m (598sq yd) upwards will have enough room for a nature pond, a refuge for many plants and creatures.
Shrubs around a pond. Only a few shrubs like to be in moist zones. They can fulfil an important function near a natural pond. If they are planted on a southern bank that is as dry as possible, they will cast some shade at midday and will ensure that the water does not warm up too much and become cloudy. The following species will do well as *solitaries* that will occasionally tolerate 'wet roots':
● weeping willow (*Salix caprea* var. 'Pendula')
● Japanese maple (*Acer palmatum*)
● Mountain snow (*Fothergilla major*, no chalk!)
● hydrangea (*Hydrangea paniculata*)
For *small groups of shrubs*, the following are very suitable:
● rose (*Rosa rugosa*), forms fat red hips
● common snowball (*Viburnum opulus*)
● hazelnut (*Corylus avellana*)
● weeping willow buddleia (*Buddleia alternifolia*)
● cherry laurel (*Prunus laurocerasus*, evergreen)
● box (*Buxus sempervirens*, evergreen).
Important: Remove fallen leaves from the pond or they will create excess fertilizer.

Perfect design

The front garden

The front garden is the showpiece of your house and its inhabitants. Remember the following, when planning:
● The front garden should complement the architecture of the house and fit into the surroundings.
● If the road that passes the house creates a lot of pollution with harmful substances and salt, choose appropriately robust plants (see page 10).
● An open front garden will look particularly friendly and will positively influence the whole look of that street. It will not, however, create a barrier to prying eyes, or to wind, dust and noise or the occasional two-legged and four-legged visitors.
An enclosed front garden is surrounded by a cut or free-growing hedge (see page 30). You should choose thorny or prickly shrubs if you require protection from undesirable visitors:
● berberis (*Berberis* species)
● hawthorn (*Crataegus* species)
● privet (*Ligustrum vulgare*, toxic!)
● blackthorn (sloe) (*Prunus spinosa*)
● hedge roses (*Rosa* species)
Important: Very small or narrow front gardens should not be closed up even more with a hedge. A fence covered with green, climbing shrubs would be a better solution.
An open front garden is not enclosed and will display its

splendour to all passers-by. There are many variations:
● An area of lawn planted with a group of shrubs or a special tree (see page 26).
● A varied group of shrubs combined with herbaceous plants on the left and the path to the front door on the right (see photo, right, with Hydrangea hybrids), cut box (*Buxus sempervirens*), a small columnar yew (*Taxus baccata 'Fatigiata Robusta'*) and hostas (*Hosta* species).
● A formal front garden (see page 32) with evergreens cut into shape.
● A heather garden (see page 35).
Your front garden will look even friendlier if you:
● Place an arch or pergola across the path to the door and allow climbing plants to grow up it.
● Flank the entrance with containers of plants.
● Create a green house wall with climbing shrubs like clematis (*Clematis* species and hybrids), *Fallopia aubertii*, ivy (*Hedera helix*, toxic!), climbing hydrangea (*Hydrangea anomala ssp. petiolaris*), winter jasmine (*Jasminum nudiflorum*), honeysuckle (*Lonicera* species), Virginia creeper (*Parthenocissus tricupidata*), climbing roses (*Rosa* species) and glycinia (*Wisteria sinensis*).
● The dustbin or its container can be covered up with a small group of shrubs.
● Create shelter for your car

with a pergola or a special tree.
My tip: Do not choose climbing plants that shed their flowers for this pergola – like glycinia (*Wisteria sinensis*) – and no species of tree that drops masses of fruit, as you could easily slip on the flowers or fruit.

A courtyard

Courtyards can often be uniform and boring, especially if they are asphalted. Even here, you may create a small, green paradise by placing dwarf shrubs in large containers, boxes and raised beds in this area.
Ideal deciduous shrubs for the purpose are box (*Buxus sempervirens*), spindle tree (*Euonymus fortunei*), shrubby cinquefoil (*Potentilla fruticosa*), dwarf almond (*Prunus tenella*), dwarf roses (*Rosa* species), dwarf willow (*Salix hastata 'Wehrhahnii'*), spiraea (*Spiraea* species) and dwarf weigela (*Weigela florida 'Purpurea'*).
Suitable coniferous shrubs: small silver fir (*Abies balsamea 'Nana'*), blue dwarf juniper (*Juniperus horizontalis 'Glauca'*), common or Norway spruce (*Picea abies 'Nidiformis'*), pine (*Pinus mugo 'Mops'*), creeping pine (*Pinus pumilo*), cushion yew (*Taxus baccata 'Repandens'*, toxic berries!), spherical cedar (*Thuja occidentalis 'Danica'*), and cushion-shaped eastern hemlock (*Tsuga canadensis*).

Open and inviting: a front garden with hydrangeas, box spheres and yew columns.

Climbing shrubs can also be grown in a trough or on an espalier. Wherever possible, the courtyard should be paved, leaving spaces for planting. You should restrict yourself to a few easy-to-care-for species of ground-cover plants and evergreen shrubs. It will all cost more money and effort if you use many shrubs and accompanying plants (see page 38) or even create a small formal garden (see page 32).

Courtyards are, as a rule, very calm. The splashing sound of a small fountain will be particularly effective and a seating area will make the courtyard a popular meeting place for friends and family (see page 28).

Perfect design

Ornamental shrubs and accompanying plants in a masterly composition.

Accompanying plants

Shrubs only display their wealth of flowers for a short while, then just the leaves and foliage remain. Attractive flowering plants or plants with interesting leaves nearby will enliven the scene and help the shrubs look more decorative. By combining different heights of growth, a spatial graduation will be achieved and gentle transitions

created. When placing shrubs and plants together, consider the requirements of the plants and their general rules of design (see page 22).

Which shrubs and plants are suitable for accompanying them? Try the following:
● semi-tall and tall herbaceous plants
● ground-covering herbaceous plants
● ferns and grasses

● bulbs and tuberous plants
● summer flowers.
Shade. The increasing shade cast by shrubs as they get older can present a problem for the accompanying plants. By choosing species that have a tendency to grow towards the light, you will save a lot of work; for example, lady's mantle (*Alchemilla mollis*) and crane's bill (*Geranium endressii*).

Remember that old bushes and trees form very tough roots, which will make planting new plants more difficult.

My tip: Do not forget to water particularly thoroughly underneath older shrubs and trees. The dense foliage will often no longer let through much rain.

Accompanying plants in the sun:

Tall and semi-tall herbaceous plants:
- campion (*Lychnis chalcedonia*)
- larkspur (*Delphinium* species and hybrids)
- garden speedwell (*Veronica* species)
- flax (*Linum* species)
- bellflower (*Campanula* species)
- rudbeckia (*Rudbeckia* species)
- rock rose (*Helianthemum* hybrids)
- globe thistle (*Echinops* species)
- yarrow, milfoil (*Achillea* species)

Bulbs and tuberous plants:
- flowering garlic (*Allium* species)
- madonna lily (*Lilium candidum*)

Accompanying plants in semi-shade:
- astilbe (*Astilbe* species and hybrids)
- bugbane, snakeroot (*Cimicifuga* species)
- columbine (*Aquilegia* species and hybrids)
- hosta (*Hosta* species)

- coral flower (*Heuchera* hybrids)
- lungwort (*Pulmonaria* species)

Accompanying plants in shade:
- deadnettle (*Lamium* species)
- creeping-Jenny (*Lysimachia* species)
- sedge (*Carex morrowii*)
- asarabacca (*Asarum europaeum*, toxic!)
- rockery astilbe (*Astilbe chinensis var. pumila*)
- barrenwort, bishop's hat (*Epimedium* species)
- hart's tongue fern (*Phyllitis scolopendrium*)
- pachysandra (*Pachysandra terminalis*, ground-covering)
- lesser periwinkle (*Vinca minor*, ground-covering)

Bulbaceous flowers, such as crocus (*Crocus* species), tulips (*Tulipa* species and hybrids), narcissus (*Narcissus* species) and scilla (*Scilla siberica*) that flower in spring can be planted without any qualms, as they will have enough light underneath deciduous shrubs and trees when they are still bare of leaves. Later, after they have withdrawn, they will no longer need light.

Unusual accompanying plants:
In the case of taller trees with not too dense foliage, such as apple (*Malus* species) and ornamental cherry (*Prunus* species), the ground beneath the tree can be framed by a round or star-shaped bed. This can be planted with herbs, vegetables, strawberries or summer flowers. Nevertheless, enough light must be able to penetrate the leafy roof.

A masterly composition

The photo, left, shows a garden designed by an expert. Elements from the formal garden (see page 32) were adapted, such as box (*Buxus sempervirens* 'Suffruticosa') edging; in other parts, beds were planted in an open design.

Shrubs and trees. A maple (*Acer negundo* 'Flamingo') was used as a solitary tree, *Floribunda* rose 'Bonica '82', and dwarf spiraea (*Spiraea japonica*).

Herbaceous plants. Giant gypsophila (*Gypsophila paniculata*), stork's bill (*Erodium manecavii*), crane's bill (*Geranium* species), acanthus (*Acanthus hungaricus*), mugwort or wormwood (*Artemisia* species), garden poppy (*Papaver orientale*), stonecrop (*Sedum telephium*), scabious (*Knautia macedonica*), *Erigeron* hybrids, garden speedwell (*Veronica longifolia*), catmint (*Napeta x faassenii*), cornflower (*Centaurea dealbata*), flowering garlic (*Allium* species), yarrow (*Achillea millefolium*), and phlox (*Phlox paniculata* hybrids).

This example has been designed elaborately, but it will give you ideas for the design of a small bed or for an underplanting of shrubs and trees.

Proper care

Ornamental shrubs and trees may become very old and still flower profusely and form fruits. The prerequisite for this is that you choose shrubs carefully, plant them in the right places and look after them properly. You will find all you need to know on the following pages.

Proper care of ornamental shrubs and trees

Top: Californian lilac, Ceanothus hybrid 'Gloire de Versailles', flowers in blue – a rare colour among ornamental shrubs.
Left: A garden pavilion in the shade of ornamental shrubs and trees is an ideal spot to have a rest after working in the garden.

Proper care

Purchasing ornamental shrubs and trees

Good quality ornamental shrubs are sold at the best nurseries. Observe the shrubs carefully before buying them and pay attention to the following:
● labels with exact species and variety names
● vigorous, undamaged growth
● free of diseases and pests
Tree nurseries will offer shrubs and trees for sale in the following state:
Stem bushes are well-branching specimens with a height of at least 2.5m (7½ft).
Tree-like plants that do not yet have a strong crown.
Standard trees have a straight, non-branching stem of at least 1.8m (6ft).
Solitaries are older trees or bushes, already displaying their typical shape of growth.
With or without a rootstock.
● Shrubs and trees with bare roots are the cheapest, but periwinkles and some other species cannot be planted in this way.
● Plants with rootstocks will cost more, as growing them is more labour-intensive.
● Container plants are even more expensive, as they are sold in plastic containers.
Planting time. Shrubs and trees with bare roots or a rootstock should be planted in spring and autumn during the rest period. Container plants can still be planted in summer, but need to be watered thoroughly.

My tip: Preferably plant only in spring or autumn, as container plants will often grow quite slowly.

Propagating shrubs and trees

Shrubs and trees can be propagated from seed (generative) or from rooting parts of plants.
   Sowing seed is a cheap method of propagation but requires patience. The seedlings will, however, often not inherit the good characteristics of their parents, and many varieties will be infertile. Seed is also difficult to buy and so much knowledge is necessary for sowing, that the second method of propagation is recommended.
Vegetative propagation will rapidly result in young plants that carry the characteristics of the mother plants. This can be carried out in different ways:
● Summer cuttings: the best time for these is late summer and early autumn. Cut off 10–15cm (4–6in) long, only slightly woody shoots, just under a leaf axil. After removing the bottom leaves or needles, dip the ends in rooting powder and then place them about 2cm (¾in) deep in a pot of cutting compost. A transparent plastic hood that can be held in place with wire or a stick will ensure the air is humid enough and will help the cutting form roots more easily.

● Autumn cuttings: this is the most frequently used method of propagating deciduous trees. In late autumn or winter, after the leaves have fallen, cut off the tip of a shoot formed this year, but woody and properly mature, and divide it into approximately 25–30cm (10–12in) long pieces with diagonal cuts. The lower surface of a cut should always be just under a bud. The small pieces of woody shoot can be bundled and pressed into moist sand for cool storage. In early spring, as soon as the ground is no longer frozen, push the individual sticks into a bed where the soil has been well loosened, with the top buds sticking out of the soil. Rooting will rapidly take place. Lilac, honeysuckle, weigela, privet, roses, deutzia, forsythia and willows can be propagated very easily in this way.
● Rhizomes: some species form underground runners called rhizomes, which grow into new plants. They can simply be separated off with a spade; the new plant is then dug up, and transplanted to the desired position. Buckthorn, robinia, elder and mountain laurel can be propagated in this way.
● Hanging shoots: shoots that are hanging near the ground can be bent down completely in early summer and fixed under the ground with a wire loop, while the tip of the shoot is above ground. Keep the shoot very moist afterwards. As soon as roots have started to form,

Box and many climbing shrubs are easy to propagate

separate the young plant from the mother plant, and transplant it to the desired position. In this way, you can propagate rhododendrons, magnolia, smoke bush, dogwood, jasmine, ornamental quince, snowball and many other climbing plants.

● Dividing: shrubs that avidly form new shoots from their rootstocks can be divided with a spade into two or more pieces, depending on their size, either in the spring or autumn. These pieces should then be planted immediately. The following plants are suitable for the procedure: rhododendron, snowy mespilus, elder, periwinkle, mahonia, berberis, spiraea, and deutzia.

Proper care

The soil

Shrubs grow best in loose, humus-rich soils that store nutrients and warmth well, and which are then accessible to plants. Good soil should consist of fine as well as coarse particles, fall into loose crumbs in your hand, contain earthworms and have a pleasant 'earthy' smell.

Types of soil. Alongside organic components such as humus, all garden soils contain mineral substances that influence the characteristics of individual soil types. Take a handful of garden soil and press it between the palms of your hands.

● A clay-rich soil is present if you can shape it into a thin 'doughy' roll, that is shiny and sticky. It will be a very heavy soil that will store a lot of water, expand, is badly aerated, and will only warm up very slowly, turns muddy in rain and forms cracks in dry spells. It does contain many nutrients but these are not readily accessible to plants. Only very few robust wild shrubs will grow on it. Before planting ornamental shrubs in this kind of soil, you will definitely need to improve it first. Dig a generous planting hole and loosen the soil two spade-depths down. Work in plenty of sand and compost in a ratio of 1:1.

● You have a loamy soil if it can be broken up into small crumbs. It is a medium-heavy, nutrient-rich soil that can store water, but is also well-aerated and warms up quickly. It is not necessary to improve it, but regular mulching (see below) is definitely recommended.

● A sandy soil is present if it cannot be shaped, and it runs through your fingers. It is a very light soil that warms up rapidly, is well aerated and easy to work. It cannot, however, hold water or nutrients well, dries out quickly, and fertilizer quickly gets washed out. Here, you should work in plenty of loam and mulch it frequently.

The pH value tells you the acidity of the soil. A neutral soil has a pH value of 7; if it is below that, the soil is acid; values above 7 indicate an alkaline, lime-rich soil. The ideal pH value for most ornamental shrub species lies between 6 and 7, that is, in the slightly acid range. Some shrubs have special requirements (see tables, pages 14-15 and 18-19). Very acid soils offer unfavourable living conditions for most plants. By adding lime, you can improve such soils. Very alkaline soils, on the other hand, contain too much chalk that binds nutrients and trace elements, so they are not available for plants. Peat substitute or real peat help to lower the pH value.

My tip: The pH value is easy to measure with an indicator stick that can be obtained in the specialist trade, or by using a special soil testing kit. You should definitely measure the pH value when a garden is newly created, and improve the soil beforehand, if necessary.

Nutrient content: Exact values are only given by a proper soil analysis carried out by professionals. It is recommended for an intensively used garden as, along with the results, you will receive recommendations for fertilizing, so you will be able to avoid mistakes. Obtain information from the institute of your choice about the exact costs and the procedure for collecting samples of soil.

Improving compacted soil: soils that have become compacted through building work need to be mechanically loosened again with a rotivator or small digger before establishing a garden. Landscape design firms can perform this task for you. Small areas can be dug over to two spade's depth in autumn. Before planting, it is a good idea to give the whole plot a basic fertilizer, by sowing phacelia (*Phacelia tanacetifolia*) or white mustard (*Sinapis alba*), scattering the seed widely. This will introduce more nitrogen to the soil and the plants' deep roots will loosen it. In the autumn, work the plants into the soil.

Improving marshy ground. This type of soil will be acid, contain a lot of peat, bind water, be nutrient-poor and can be squeezed together like a sponge. It is very suitable for plants like rhododendron, but most other shrubs will not thrive in it. In order to improve it, mix in sand, loam, compost and chalk.

Creating marsh-like conditions. Rhododendrons require more elaborate preparations if they are to be planted in lime-rich or chalky soil:

● Dig a hole twice as deep and wide as needed for the rootstock.

● Place a 20cm (8in) thick layer of rhododendron special compost into the hole, stand the rootstock in it and fill up the rest of the hole with special soil.

● Later, regularly add a 20cm (8in) thick peat layer to the area around the roots.

Mulching

This term denotes covering up the surface of the ground with organic material, such as ripe compost, well-rotted manure, dead leaves, bark, dried grass cuttings, cuttings from deciduous hedge trimming or straw. The layer should be about 4–6cm (1½–2in) thick. Healthy, fallen autumn leaves from your ornamental shrubs make an excellent material for mulching. Only leaves that contain a lot of tannin, like those of chestnut, oak, and walnut, are not suitable for this purpose.

The mulching layer will help to:
● keep the moisture in the soil and decrease the need for watering
● balance the temperatures in the soil
● prevent damage from frost
● support the survival of valuable soil organisms
● improve fertile soil
● subdue undesirable weeds
● avoid erosion by rain and wind.

Rhododendrons need acid soil.

45

Practise: planting shrubs and trees

The way to proceed will depend on what species you have bought and whether the roots of the plants are bare or come with a rootstock.

Watering shrubs and trees
Illustration 1

Shrubs with bare roots may easily dry out. Stand them in a bucket of water for a few hours as soon as you get them home. If you do not have time to plant them right away, temporarily heel in the roots in the garden, after having watered them well beforehand, and then keep them evenly moist.

Planting cut
Illustration 2

Rotted or bent roots should be cut off cleanly. Generally shorten the roots by about a third, as this will encourage new growth of the hair roots. To balance this, for most deciduous types, also cut back the crown shoots by a third. Summer flowering species like the blue spiraea (*Caryopteris x clandonensis*), hydrangea (*Hydrangea* species) and the butterfly tree (*Buddleia* species) should be shortened to a shoot length of 30cm (12in).

My tip: In a tree nursery, you will be able to have the planting cut done for you when you buy the plants.

Planting climbing shrubs against a wall
Illustration 3

First fix the climbing aid to the wall. Then dig the planting hole at a distance of about 20cm (8in) from the wall and protect this from wetness with a layer of gravel – possibly with a piece of liner. Climbing shrubs are often supplied in containers. Remove the shrub's rootstock from the container and cut it back, if necessary. Place the rootstock in a slightly inclined position so that the plant parts above ground are leaning towards the climbing aid. Fill the hole with soil. If necessary, tie the shoots to the climbing aid. The wall will give off warmth, so regular watering will be required. Proceed in the same way when planting climbing shrubs for free-standing climbing aids. First anchor the structure firmly in the ground.

3 Planting climbing shrubs against a wall.

Planting roses
Illustration 4

Roses root deeply, so you will need to make the planting hole deep enough that the grafting point – visible by a thickening above the rootstock – lies about 5cm (2in) below the surface of the soil. Fill the hole with soil and press down to form a watering 'gully'. Water thoroughly.

1 Watering roots before planting.

2 The planting cut of bare roots.

Piling up soil around roses
Illustration 5

Freshly planted roses and those that are established should have some soil heaped up around them to protect them from frost and from drying out. As soon as new shoots appear in the spring, remove the excess soil again and distribute it around the plants.

Planting a tree
Illustrations 6–9

Proceed in the following sequence:
● Prepare the planting hole (see illustration 6): Dig out the planting hole, twice as big as the rootstock or the rootball. Thoroughly loosen the bottom layer of soil, and enrich the soil with a few shovelfuls of ripe compost. Do not use mineral fertilizer or fresh manure as this would damage the roots. If a prop is needed, ram it in before planting, so it cannot damage the roots of the plant.
● Plant the tree (see illustration 7). Place the plant straight upright in the centre of the hole, add a bit of soil, lift the plant slightly and shake it, so that all the hollows around the roots are filled with soil. Finally, tie the plant to the prop with a length of coconut rope twisted in a figure '8' shape. Do not plant too deeply: the top edge of the rootstock should be level with the surface of the ground. Finally, fill up the planting hole with soil and carefully tread down the soil to

4 Planting and watering roses.

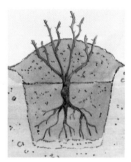

5 Piling up soil around roses in the autumn.

form a watering 'gully'.
Important: If the rootstock is enveloped in a piece of cloth, knot it up above the neck of the root, as it will eventually rot away.
● Water the tree (see illustration 8): Immediately after planting, especially if there is a dry period, water very thoroughly by filling the area around the planted tree right up to the top of

the 'gully'. Use a gentle stream of water.
● Mulch the circle of ground around the tree (see illustration 9). Add a thick mulching layer, for example made of chopped bark (see page 45). It will rot away gradually and can then be worked into the soil. Renew the mulching layer regularly.

6 Digging a planting hole, ramming in a stake.

7 Planting a tree and tying it to a stake.

8 Watering the freshly planted tree.

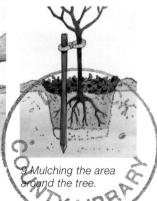

9 Mulching the area around the tree.

Proper care

Cut at the right time with good tools: an evergreen oasis.

Shaping

A shaping cut will maintain the plant's willingness to form flowers, the plant will be encouraged to put out vigorous new growth, and the shrub will be prevented from aging prematurely. It is very important to use the right tools and to do this job at the right time. The basic rules for cutting can be found on the following page.

The right tools

You will find a large selection of the correct tools in the specialist trade:

● Secateurs are suitable for cutting young shoots to a thickness of about 2cm (1in).
● Larger secateurs with strong handles for cutting thick branches will manage to cut branches up to a thickness of about 5cm (2in).

● A tree saw, or even better an adjustable bow saw, will cope with large branches.
● A pruning knife, a sharp knife with a curved blade, is used for cleaning up sawn cuts.
● A hedge trimmer makes exact cutting and trimming of hedges much easier.
Important: All tools need to be sharpened, so that the cuts are clean and smooth.

Protection against accidents

Always wear tough garden gloves to protect yourself against accidents. Never work with half-rusty, blunt tools, as this will easily cause accidents that might result in septicemia.
Use only ladders that have a British Standards kite mark and always pay attention to safety instructions.

When to cut?

Species that flower in summer and autumn should be cut on a frost-free day in spring. Shrubs that flower in spring, on the other hand, that have formed buds the year before, should be cut after they have flowered, otherwise you will deprive yourself of the flower display. Hedges should preferably not be cut before the end of the first month of summer, so they do not immediately produce vigorous new growth.

Special case: roses

Depending on their growth and use, roses will require an appropriate cut in spring.
● Bedding roses would grow too tall without being cut back and would not flower very much.
● Bedding roses that do not grow very much should be cut back to 3–4 buds per shoot (10–15cm/4–6in tall).

● Leave at least three buds on each shoot, as the rose would otherwise shoot rather late. This is because the shoots come out of the buds that sit further down, the 'sleeping eyes', and will only develop very slowly.
● Medium vigorous bedding roses should be cut back to 4–6 buds (15–25cm/6–10in tall).
● Vigorously growing bedding roses should be cut back to 8 buds.
● Completely remove any shoots that have died in the frost.
My tip: If a rose looks dead, cut it back to just above the ground; 'sleeping eyes' might still put forth new shoots.
Bedding roses – summer cut: Shoots that have finished flowering should be cut back by 2-3 sets of leaves in all rose species that flower several times a year (*Remontant* roses); this is in order to avoid the formation of hips that sap energy, and to initiate vigorous new growth.
Important: A summer cut is not recommended for varieties that bloom only once, as the hips are desirable for their ornamental value.
Cutting climbing roses: Leave the thick main shoots standing that form the frame on an espalier. The side shoots, however, can be cut back to about 3–4 buds. These will develop into the flower buds.
Cutting standard roses: Similarly to bedding roses, they will need a vigorous cutting

back, to form a bushy, compact crown. Climbing rose varieties grafted onto a standard, that form a crown that hangs down in a cascade, will only receive a thinning out cut (see Practise, page 50).

Cutting a hedge

Hedges made of shrubs that can stand cutting, like box (*Buxus sempervirens*), yew (*Taxus baccata*), false cypress (*Chamaecyparis* species), berberis (*Berberis julianiae*), privet (*Ligustrum* species) and hornbeam (*Carpinus betulus*, for hedges, see also pages 30–1), are best cut in a trapeze shape – that is, wider at the bottom than at the top – so the lower parts get more light. Do not cut into the old wood of conifers, as the hedge would easily go bare, and gaps would ensue. Only yew (*Taxus baccata*) will put out new shoots after such radical cutting. Cutting back to just above the previous year's new growth will lead to increased new growth that is compact and luxuriant. A string and a batten are practical, helpful aids with which to mark out the desired shape.

Practise: cutting

Proper cutting is not difficult. Provided you use the right equipment, choose the right time (see pages 48–9) and keep to the following basic rules.

Cutting shoots
Illustration 1

The cut should be made about 0.5–1cm (⅕–⅖in) above a bud pointing outwards. The surface of the cut should slope upwards towards the outside. This will prevent rainwater from penetrating the bud and causing decay. The distance from the bud should be no greater because otherwise, an ugly stump will be left that will decay. The bud

might dry out if the cut is too close above it.

Taking out branches
Illustrations 2 to 4

Large branches have a considerable weight of their own and would break off and splinter if they were sawn too close to the trunk. This would result in large wounds that the tree would find difficult to heal. To avoid this, proceed as follows:
● About 20cm (8in) from the trunk, begin to saw through half the branch, from below.
● Another 10cm (4in) further out, make a second cut from above and saw the branch, until it collapses under its own weight and breaks off to the first cut.

● Now, saw off the stump as smoothly as possible at the trunk.
● If necessary, cut off frayed surfaces with a special pruning knife and remove loose pieces of bark. Use tree wax to cover the cut surface and protect it from organisms that might make the tree diseased. Even large cut surfaces can heal in this way.

Regular, shaping cut
Illustration 5

Regularly thinning out shrubs from the start, to train a shaped crown that is open to light, will mean that you do not need to make larger, time- and effort-consuming corrections later on. The shrub will reward you with a profusion of flowers.

1 Expertly cutting off shoots.

This is how to proceed:
● Always cut above a bud pointing outwards. Its new growth will result in a more open structure of the bush.
● Dead shoots that have grown inwards and crossed over with others should be taken out.
● Cut diseased parts right back into healthy wood.
● Wood that can no longer support flowers should be removed

5 The 'building-up' cut requires only minor cutting of the peripheral area of the bush.

6 The thinning-out cut requires more radical cutting right into the centre of the bush.

completely or taken out above a fork.

Important: The stronger the cutting back, the more vigorous the new growth. Do not overdo things as the growth typical for the species should be maintained.

Thinning out cut
Illustration 6

After a few years, many shrubs begin to grow too densely and you will need to cut more radically.

● For species whose shoots come up directly out of the ground as, for example, with hazelnut (*Corylus avellana*), deutzia (*Deutzia gracilis*) and weigela (*Weigela* hybrids), you may remove the oldest ground shoots right at the base, so that young

2 Cut off larger branches in stages.

wood can shoot up from below. Still allow several older ground shoots to remain.

● Bushes and semi-bushes that flower from one-year-old shoots should be cut about two hand widths above the ground, so that they will be encouraged to produce vigorous shoots and numerous flowers. Among these are blue spiraea (*Caryopteris x clandonensis*),

3 Saw off the stump of the branch near the trunk.

ceanothus (*Ceanothus* hybrids), St John's wort (*Hypericum calycinum*) and spiraea (*Spiraea albiflora* and other species and hybrids).

Rejuvenating cut
Illustration 7

If a shrub has not been cut for years, has become very bare, and is no longer growing or producing flowers, a radical cut back in late autumn is recommended:

Bushes. The old, senile shoots should be cut off about 30-40cm (12–16in) above the ground, so that new vigorous growth can result from below.

Trees. Cut off the oldest branches of the crown just above a fork

4 Carefully smooth off the edges of the cut.

and towards a younger shoot pointing outwards.

7 The rejuvenating cut should be fairly radical; cut back to just above the ground.

Proper care

Encouraging resistance and useful creatures

Prevention is better than cure so, in principle, choose shrubs that will thrive in the conditions present in your garden. Indigenous trees and shrubs are less susceptible than those from foreign climate zones. A good, crumbly, humus-rich soil, with active soil organisms and a covering layer of mulch, as well as sufficient water and nutrients, will produce strong plants and render them more resistant.

Important: Advice on the most common diseases and pests and how to combat them can be found on the following double pages. Not every aphid means your shrubs are immediately subject to a life-endangering threat and therefore require severe measures. In nature, there are many useful creatures, the natural enemies that eat pests. They will only appear, however, if you tolerate a minimum of pests – otherwise, they would have no real basis for food and would die of starvation. Ladybirds, lacewings, hoverflies, earwigs, spiders and birds will do their best to help you by eating aphids and other insects. Toads, frogs and hedgehogs love slugs and snails, larvae and caterpillars.

Encouraging helpful creatures. These creatures will prefer niches in your garden that are not too tidy and orderly. Hedgehogs like piles of branches and hedge trimmings that are ideal for overwintering. A flower-pot turned upside down and filled with wood shavings and then tied up in a tree will provide earwigs, that are active at night, with a place to sleep in the daytime. Nesting boxes placed in tall bushes and trees offer breeding places for birds. Bundles of reeds or chunks of wood with holes bored in them will provide winter quarters for ichneumon flies.

Environmentally friendly substances

Plant extracts may be used as prevention against diseases, as they fortify the cell tissue and have a germicidal effect. They will also help with infestations of disease or pests. A more precise list is given in the table opposite. There are four ways of manufacturing these extracts:
● For brews, leave the plant parts to soak in cold water for a day, and then boil it all up.
● Brew teas like a herb tea, and allow it to sit for 15 minutes.
● For a cold water extract, soak fresh or dried leaves in water, and allow it to stand for 1-3 days. It should not start to ferment. Then spray it undiluted.
● Fermented brews should be prepared in the same way, but will have to stand and ferment for 10–14 days, then spray after diluting.

Spraying: The extracts, prepared as described above, should be skimmed off. Then use a hose to spray them over the affected plants. The plant matter left over after preparation can be used as mulching matter.

A soft soap solution is good for combatting aphids and is non-toxic. Depending on the degree of infestation, dissolve 150 to 300g (3½–7oz) pure soft soap from the chemists in a bucket with 10 litres (17 pints) of hot water and allow to cool. Then spray undiluted over infested plants.

Algae powder and stonemeal are good against moulds that have colonized the excretions of aphids.

Paraffin oil preparations are used as sprays. They are non-toxic to humans, cover pests, their eggs and larvae with a film of oil and suffocate them. As this will also kill useful insects, only employ paraffin oil if the infestation is severe.

Pyrethrum preparations used against insects are considered to be ecologically 'non-toxic'. They do, however, also affect useful insects and may even cause allergic reactions in sensitive people. Restrict their use to cases of dire need.

Protecting plants with other plants

Plant	Ingredients for	Preparation/ mixture	Use/dilution	Effect
comfrey	10 litres (17 pints) 1kg (2lb) fresh leaves or 150g (5oz) dried plant parts	fermented brew mixed with nettles	liquid fertilizer, 1:10 during the whole vegetation period	generally fortifies plants; rich in potash
stinging nettle	1kg (2lb) fresh leaves or 150g (5oz) dried plant parts	fermented brew mixed with comfrey, mare's tail, cold water extract	liquid fertilizer 1:10 leaf spray 1:20 undiluted	generally fortifies plants and wards off insects; against aphids
fern (male fern)	1kg (2lb) fresh leaves or 100g (3½oz) dried plant parts	fermented brew or brew	in early spring spray 1:10	against different species of aphids
tansy	300g (10oz) fresh leaves or 30g (1oz) dried plant parts	tea, mixed with mare's tail tea	winter spray undiluted over plants, summer spray on leaves and ground, 1:2 – 1:3	against mites and other pests; against rusty mould and mildew
mare's tail	1kg (2lb) fresh plant parts or 150g (5oz) dried plant parts	brew or fermented brew, mixed with nettles	spring to late summer, if poss. on sunny mornings, 1:5	fortifies resistance against fungal infections like mildew, scales, rust, and leaf spot diseases
wormwood	300g (10oz) fresh plant parts or 30g (1oz) dried plant parts	tea / fermented brew	in spring, undiluted over the plants, in summer 1:3 in autumn 1:2	against ants, aphids, caterpillars; also against rust; spray in summer and autumn against aphids and moths
onions and/or garlic	500g (1lb) onions and/or garlic	fermented brew, mixed with a few leaves of blackcurrant	pour on the ground around the tree, 1:10	fortifies resistance to fungal infections
tomatoes	2 handfuls small shoots or leaves per 2–3 litres (3½–5 pints)	cold water extract, pressed plant parts, allow to draw for 3 hours	water plants, undiluted	against caterpillars

Proper care

Identifying damage

Even healthy shrubs are not completely immune to pests and diseases. Check the plants regularly, therefore, so you can act in time. Damage can only be alleviated if you are able to identify the perpetrator without any doubt. First of all, exclude the possibility that it might be a mistake in care or the result of extreme weather conditions. If you are not sure about the cause, you might want to turn to a specialist.

Simple measures for combatting problems

It is not always necessary to reach for chemicals. Often, the use of plant extracts (see page 53) will be quite adequate. Simply picking off the pests by hand or attaching sticky rings to the stem or bark will often yield good results. Fungal infections, like grey mould, mildew and rust, can be combatted by cutting back to healthy wood. Destroy the infested parts of the plant; do not compost them. Consistently sickly shrubs should be replaced by robuster ones.

The five most common pests

Aphids
Damage: green, pinkish red, brown or black insects sit on leaves, shoots or flowers which are crinkly. *Remedy:* spray with soft soap solution or with plant extracts (see page 53). Encourage useful insects and other creatures.

Scale insects
Damage: Sticky leaves and falling leaves. Small brownish scales, under which the insects sit, appear on leaves and shoots. *Remedy:* brush off the scales, spray with soft soap solution, spray with paraffin oil if badly infested.

Vine weevil
Damage: Eaten pieces missing from leaves; sawlike bite edges from black beetles; larvae in the ground eat the roots; the plants wither and die. *Remedy:* collect beetles and larvae. Spray with wormwood extract (see page 53).

Mealy bug
Damage: Insects covered in cotton wool-like, whiteish, waxy excretions sit on leaves and shoots. *Remedy:* brush off the 'cotton wool' and then spray with a soft soap solution; if heavily infested, use paraffin oil.

Spider mite
Damage: Miniscule white or red mites on needles and the undersides of leaves. Needles and leaves display yellow dots and are covered in fine, web-like filaments. *Remedy:* Spray shoots with paraffin oil, then later with pyrethrum preparations.

Chemical sprays

If infestation of a plant has reached the point where damage is appearing, chemical agents can be used, once the cause has been identified without doubt. The agents, as well as advice and help, can be obtained from the specialist garden trade. In general, observe the following:

● Keep to the instructions for use.
● Use the recommended concentration.
● Work with gloves and protective clothing.
● Do not inhale the fine spray.
● Do not eat or smoke while spraying.
● Do not spray into opened flowers.
● Treat the undersides of leaves as well as the tops.
● Clean the spraying equipment thoroughly, immediately after use.
● Store the agents in their original containers, never together with food, always closed or sealed, and inaccessible to children or pets.
● Do not pour away any remainders. They have to be disposed of as special waste.

The five most common diseases

Grey mould
Damage: Leaves, flowers and shoots hang limply down, in spite of sufficient moisture, and are covered with a grey film. *Remedy:* cut out infested shoots back to the healthy wood and destroy the pieces.

Genuine mildew
Damage: A white, flour-like, wipeable film on leaves, flowers and young shoots. *Remedy:* Cut back shoots into the healthy wood and destroy the pieces. Spray with tansy extract (see page 53).

False mildew
Damage: A dirty, whiteish film on the undersides of leaves; the leaves turn grey and drop off. *Remedy:* Cut back the infested shoots into the healthy wood and destroy the infested pieces. Spray with tansy extract (see page 53).

Rust
Damage: Yellow or red, later black pustules on bark, rusty red spots on leaves. *Remedy:* Cut back infested shoots into the healthy wood and destroy the infested parts. Spray with tansy extract (see page 53).

Fireblight
Damage: Flowers turn black. The shoots are twisted in hook-like shapes and dry out. Yellowish bacterial slime on the bark. *Remedy:* Burn the plant.

Proper care

An ABC of shrub care

Looking after ornamental shrubs and trees, watering, fertilizing them properly and getting them through the winter is not very difficult. If you keep to the following advice, you will have many years of joy with your plants.

Watering

Freshly planted shrubs and trees require particularly thorough watering, as they are supposed to form fine hair roots as soon as possible. During their first year, especially during the summer months, water them regularly. Further important points are:

● Allow water to soak away slowly, using a gently running stream of water. A hard jet of water from a garden hose that washes away soil and exposes the roots is damaging to the shrubs and bushes.

● Evergreen shrubs and trees should, in principle, be watered in winter too, provided the ground is not frozen, as they lose water through evaporation all year round.

● Older, well-rooted bushes and trees will only require watering after lengthy dry periods. Give them a good heavy soaking.

● Very dense foliage will often not let any water through to the roots, even in heavy rain. These shrubs and trees definitely need watering.

● The best time for watering in summer is during the morning or evening. In the midday heat, large quantities of water evaporate and the leaves may burn.

● Soft rainwater, that has been allowed to stand for a while, is much more suitable for watering plants than hard water containing a lot of calcium.
My tip: Before watering rhododendrons, hang a small sack filled with peat in the watering can for a few hours. This will soften the water.

Fertilizing

Most shrubs and trees are quite frugal with respect to fertilizer, provided they grow in a nutrient-rich, normal garden soil. Mulching and additional doses of compost will generally be sufficient. Shortly after planting, no mineral fertilizers should, in principle, be worked in, as they would lead to damage to the roots. Fresh manure too would cause damage. Vigorously growing climbing plants or hedges that are shooting, rhododendrons and conifers do, however, need doses of fertilizer.

● Organic fertilizer, like hornmeal, bonemeal and guano, should be spread in the autumn, as they require a long time to become accessible for the plants.

● On the other hand, organic-mineral fertilizers should be added in the spring.

● Special fertilizers like Epsom salts or potash-magnesium compounds will help overcome a lack of the element magnesium. This problem often occurs with coniferous shrubs and trees that start to have yellow needles. There are various brand name products that will help with this condition.

● Always water well after using fertilizer, as this will make the absorption of nutrients easier for plants.

● Never use a higher than recommended concentration, as this will lead to over-fertilizing and could harm the plants.
Types of fertilizer. Garden centres sell fertilizers in the form of powders, granules or liquids. The liquid fertilizers work fastest and they should be used if a shrub or tree is suffering from acute nutrient deficiency.
Hardiness to freezing conditions. The last fertilizing of the summer should be carried out no later than the end of the second month of summer. Otherwise, nitrogen in particular will cause the shrub or tree to form further new growth and these late shoots are more susceptible to sucking insects, fungal infections and frost. In regions with hard winters, we recommend using a potash fertilizer in the first month of autumn, as this encourages resistance to frost.

Roses and clematis: thriving, thanks to fertilizer and winter protection.

Winter protection

Most indigenous trees and bushes in our climate are hardy. In extreme winters, one or the other shrub or tree may suffer frost damage, so cut back the plant into the healthy wood in the spring.

● Roses are often sensitive to frost. Bedding roses should be partially covered with soil, in order to protect the grafting point, and then covered up with coniferous branches for protection. Standard roses, while young and still flexible, should be bent down by their cut crowns and covered up with conifer branches or other brushwood. Older specimens can be protected by tying brushwood firmly around the crown.

● Rhododendrons are sensitive to exposed positions. A simple wooden frame covered all over with brushwood will provide excellent protection.
● Thick, wet and heavy layers of snow should be removed from broad, spreading coniferous branches, as they may cause the branches to break off.

Index

Index

Index

Index

Author's notes

This volume deals with the planting and care of ornamental shrubs and trees, as well as with their propagation. Some of the plants described here have varying degrees of toxicity. Lethally toxic plants and those that are toxic enough to cause considerable health problems in adults or children have been marked with a skull and crossbones in the tables on pages 14–15 and 18–19. Make absolutely sure that children and pets do not consume any of these. Wear gloves when handling and cutting thorny shrubs, to prevent injury. Keep your garden tools in a safe place, so that no one can injure themselves on them. Consult your physician as soon as possible and get expert advice if you suffer an injury when handling soil. Discuss whether it is advisable to have a tetanus injection.

All fertilizers and plant protection agents, even environmentally friendly ones, should be stored in such a way that they are inaccessible to children and pets. The consumption of these substances may damage your health. Also ensure that none of these products or substances get into anyone's eyes.

Cover photographs

Front cover: main, Star Jasmine; inset top, honeysuckle; inset middle, lilac; inset bottom, cherry blossom.
Back cover: Clematis

Photographic acknowledgements:

Becker: Inside front cover, page 2, 4/5, 5 right, 7, 21 right, 23, 34 bottom, 38, 43, 48, 57;
Borstell: p. 16 bottom right, 20/21, 29 bottom, 33 top, 34 top, 37, 64/inside back cover, back cover top left, top right;
Garden Picture Library: front cover, main;
Merehurst Picture Library: front cover, top and middle insets, back cover;
Morell: back cover bottom;
Murdoch Books Picture Library: front cover, bottom inset;
Nickig: p. 3 left, 16 centre right, 27, 29 top left, top right, centre right, 33 bottom, 45;
Redeleit: front cover (small photo);
Reinhard: front cover (large photo), p. 3 right, 11, 12 top left, bottom left, centre right, bottom right, 13 top, bottom left, 16 bottom left, 17 top, bottom left, bottom right, 29 centre left, 40/41;
Reinhard, Nils: p. 16 top right;
Schneiders, U.: p. 29 centre;
Stehling: p. 12 top right;
Strauss: p. 16 top left, 31, 41 right;
Willer, W: p. 13 bottom right

This edition published 2001 by Murdoch Books UK Ltd, Ferry House, 51–57 Lacy Road, Putney, London SW15 1PR

ISBN 1–85391–950 0

© 1997 Gräfe and Unzer Verlag GmbH, Munich

English text copyright © Murdoch Books UK Ltd 2000
Translated by Astrid Mick
Typesetting and editorial by Grapevine Publishing Services Ltd
Printed in Hong Kong by Wing King Tong

Autumn splendour in a front garden

There are no bounds to the imagination when you are creating interesting combinations of ornamental shrubs. You can play about with a great variety of colours. At the end of summer when few plants are still flowering, we enter the period of colourful leaves and brilliantly coloured fruit and berries. Evergreen species provide the central, stable feature, a dark background in front of which other colours begin to glow. Attractive decorative accessories like the stone sphere (see photo right) enhance the charm of a planting arrangement.

This well-conceived plantation glows in wonderful complementary colours in the autumn. The dark evergreen shrubs ivy, box, yew and skimmia set off the autumn colouring of the creeper.